Looking at
Trees
and
Leaves

Library of Congress Cataloging-in-Publication Data

Bergen, Lara Rice.
  Looking at trees and leaves / by Lara Bergen ; illustrated by Claudia Karabaic
Sargent and Tim Haggerty.
    p. cm. — (My first field guides)
  Summary: An elementary field guide to leaves and trees including a leaf
identification chart and stickers.
  ISBN 0-448-42517-3
    1. Trees—Juvenile literature. 2. Leaves—Juvenile literature. [1. Trees. 2. Leaves.] I.
Sargent, Claudia Karabaic, ill. II. Haggerty, Tim, ill. III. Title. IV. Series.

QK475.8.B47 2001
582.16—dc21   2001045203

Photo credits: cover (white oak) Photo Researchers Inc. © Michael Gadomski; (beech)
Photo Researchers Inc. © Michael Gadomski; (maple) EARTH SCENES © Donald Specker;
(honey locust) EARTH SCENES © Phil Degginger; (red oak) Photo Researchers Inc. ©
Michael Gadomski; (fir) Photo Researchers Inc. © Jerry Ferrara; p. 8 Photo Researchers
Inc. © Renee Lynn; p. 21 Photo Researchers Inc. © Michael Gadomski; p. 23 Photo
Researchers Inc. © Michael Gadomski; p. 25 EARTH SCENES © John Lemker;
p. 27 EARTH SCENES © E.R. Degginger; p. 29 EARTH SCENES © Donald Specker;
p. 31 EARTH SCENES © Don Enger; p. 33 EARTH SCENES © Michael Habicht; p. 35
Photo Researchers Inc. © Adam Jones; p. 37 Photo Researchers Inc. © Leonard Lee Rue III;
p. 39 Photo Researchers © E.R. Degginger; p. 41 EARTH SCENES © Richard Shiell; p. 43
EARTH SCENES © Leonard Lee Rue III; p. 45 Photo Researchers Inc. © Adam Jones;
p. 47 EARTH SCENES © Richard Kolar.

ISBN 0-448-42517-3   A B C D E F G H I J

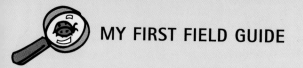

Looking at Trees and Leaves

By Lara Bergen

Illustrated by Claudia Karabaic Sargent
and Tim Haggerty

Grosset & Dunlap • New York

This is a leaf.
It grew on a tree.
Then fall came
and it drifted
to the ground.

This is a leaf, too.
But it looks very different.
Why?
Because it came from
a different tree.

There are many kinds of trees—
more than 50,000!
How can you tell them apart?
One way is by their leaves.

 Here are some other ways to tell trees apart:

 fruit   cones   seeds   flowers

Going on a Leaf Hunt

You can find leaves anywhere.
On your street. In the park.
In your yard. In the woods.
Here is what you need:

___ long pants and a T-shirt
    (with long sleeves if you are in the woods)
___ boots or tough shoes
___ a hat if it's hot
___ water (just in case you get thirsty!)
___ paper to wrap around the leaves
___ a folder with pockets for your leaves
___ a pencil
___ this book!

How to Use This Book

When you find a leaf,
see if it is on your ID card.
Then find the pages in the book
about that leaf.
Put your sticker on the page.

 Always look for leaves on the ground.
Don't pick them off a tree. The tree still
needs them. And so do the bugs and
caterpillars that call the leaves home!

But maybe you can't tell what leaf it is.
Just mark it with a number using
a little strip of tape.
Write the number
on the tape, and
also write the
number on a blank
page in the back of
this book.
Your page can look like this:

Today's date: September 3

Leaf number: 1

Kind of leaf: ???

Shape: Round

Size: Small

Where I found it: At the park

My notes: The leaf is light green and has spikey
edges

Maybe a teacher or other grown-up
can tell you more about the leaf later.
Remember, there are lots and lots
of different trees in the world.
You might find a leaf
that does not look like any
of the leaves in this book.
But if it is pretty close
to one you see here,
it is probably a "cousin."

It's easy to find leaves.
Just open your eyes and look around.
So turn the page to get started!

Many Shapes and Sizes

Each kind of tree has
a different kind of leaf.
Leaves come in all
shapes and sizes.

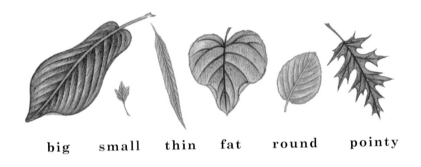

big   small   thin   fat   round   pointy

Some leaves have smooth edges.
And some have pointy <u>teeth</u>.
Other leaves have big bumps called <u>lobes</u>.

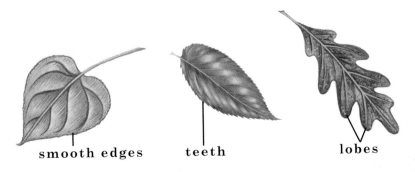

smooth edges   teeth   lobes

Some leaves are <u>simple</u>.
This means they are
made up of just one leaf.

Others are made up
of many small leaves.
These are called
<u>compound</u> leaves.

Leaves can also be long
and thin like little <u>needles</u>.

Or they can be short
and look like fish <u>scales</u>.

Parts of a Leaf

A leaf's body has many parts.

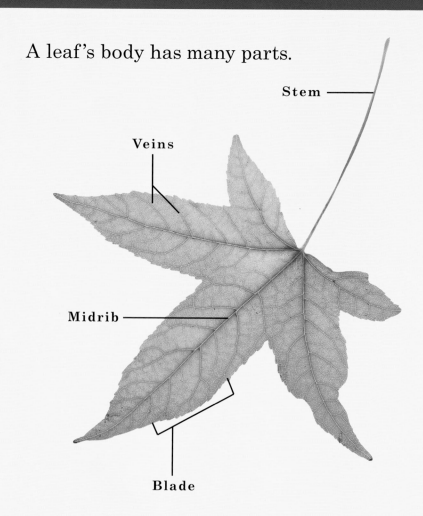

Stem

Veins

Midrib

Blade

Your veins carry blood through your body. Leaves have veins, too! They carry food and water through the leaf.

Leave It to You

Find a leaf with a long stem.
Put it in a glass of water.
Add a drop of food color.
What happens
after an hour?

Little Leaves Feed Big Trees

Leaves are pretty.
But they also help trees grow.
Leaves use energy from the sun
to turn air and water
into food for the tree.

Of course, trees are not
the only things with leaves.
All plants have leaves.

Blades of grass are leaves,

grass

and so is lettuce.

Here are other plants
with leaves:

lettuce

pineapple

potatoes

ivy

carrots

Why Leaves Fall

Some leaves change color
and fall off a tree.
Why?
In the fall, days get shorter.
There is less sunlight.
It is time for the tree
to stop growing and rest.
The healthy green color
of the leaves fades.
Other colors show through.
Slowly, the leaves dry up and fall off.
Now the leaf is dead.

But the tree is still alive.
And in the spring it
will grow new leaves!

Leave It to You

See for yourself what happens
when a leaf gets less sun.
Take some foil.
Cover a leaf on a tree
or on a plant.
Leave the foil on it for a day.
Then take off the foil.
What happened to the leaf?

 Some trees keep their
green leaves all winter.
These are called evergreens.

Needles and Scales

Some trees have needle and scalelike leaves. These can be hard to collect. Most do not fall off in the winter. Still, they are fun to look at!

Pines, firs, spruces, and larches have needles.

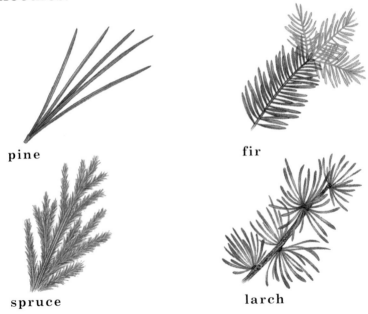

pine

fir

spruce

larch

Cypress, junipers, and cedars
all have scalelike leaves.

cypress

juniper

cedar

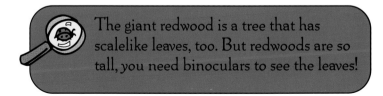

The giant redwood is a tree that has
scalelike leaves, too. But redwoods are so
tall, you need binoculars to see the leaves!

Dogwood

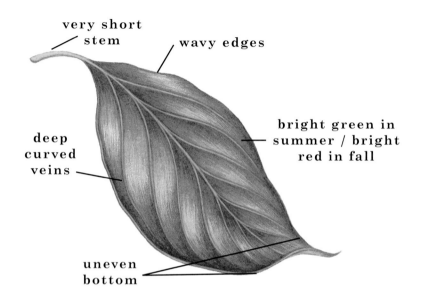

very short stem

wavy edges

bright green in summer / bright red in fall

deep curved veins

uneven bottom

It is easy to tell a dogwood tree in the spring. Just look for lots of flowers with four white or pink petals. In the fall, look for bunches of red berries and bright red leaves.

Leave It to You

Here is one way to keep
your leaves and show them off:
Slip a leaf inside a newspaper.
Then put a heavy book on top.
Every day, turn the newspaper over.
In a week, take out your leaf.
It should be dry and flat.
Glue it to a piece of
thick paper or
cardboard.

I saw a
dogwood

place your
sticker here

Willow

long, thin
blade

tiny
teeth

bright green in
summer / yellow
in fall

pointy tip

If you find a leaf that
is long and thin and
pointy and has very tiny teeth,
it could be from a willow tree.
This leaf is from a weeping willow.
Why is it called a weeping willow?
Because its branches droop
as if they are sad!

I saw a
willow

place your
sticker here

Cherry

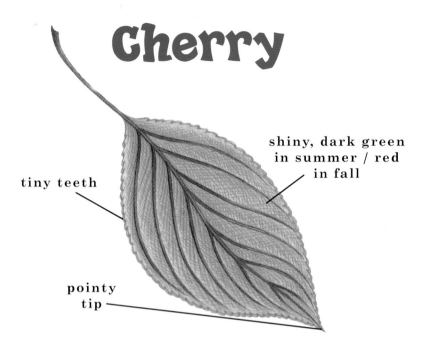

shiny, dark green in summer / red in fall

tiny teeth

pointy tip

You can tell a cherry tree by its fruit. But you can also tell one by its shiny, dark green leaves. The fruit of a cherry tree is sweet. But the leaves and bark are not. Never eat fruit, berries, or nuts from any tree unless a grown-up tells you it's okay.

I saw a
cherry

place your
sticker here

Beech

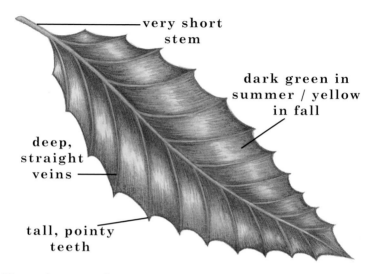

very short
stem

dark green in
summer / yellow
in fall

deep,
straight
veins

tall, pointy
teeth

Beech tree leaves are easy to spot.
In the fall, the leaves turn yellow.
Prickly burrs fall from the tree.
Look inside and you will find
two or three tiny beechnuts.
Remember: don't eat <u>anything</u> you find,
unless a grown-up says it's okay.

Leave It to You

Here is another way
to keep a leaf:
Press it in soft clay
then pull it off carefully.
Write the name of the leaf
with a stick.

I saw a
beech

place your
sticker here

Elm

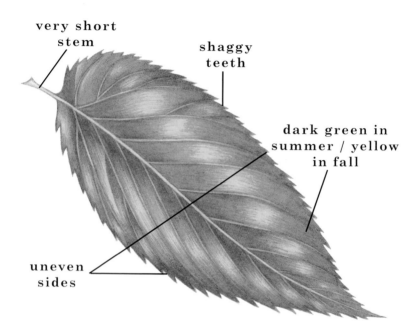

very short stem

shaggy teeth

dark green in summer / yellow in fall

uneven sides

There is something funny about this leaf.
The two sides are not the same.
And the teeth are sharp and shaggy.
Elm trees also have flat, papery seeds.

Leave It to You

Put one leaf (or more)
on newspaper.
Cover it with a thin
sheet of paper.
Then gently rub a crayon over it.
See what "magically" appears!

I saw an
elm

place your
sticker here

Paper Birch

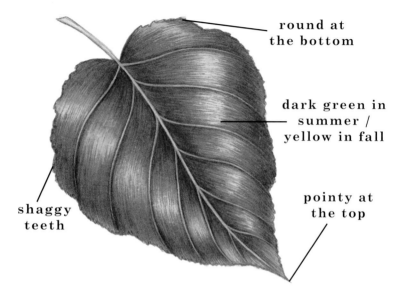

round at
the bottom

dark green in
summer /
yellow in fall

shaggy
teeth

pointy at
the top

This leaf is from a paper birch tree.
It's called that because its bark is thin
and white like paper. Sometimes
early settlers wrote on it when
they had no paper. And
Native Americans used
the waterproof bark
to cover their canoes.

I saw a
paper birch

place your
sticker here

sassafras

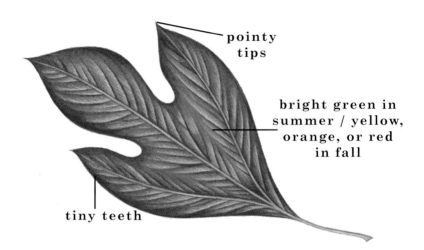

pointy
tips

bright green in
summer / yellow,
orange, or red
in fall

tiny teeth

Sassafras leaves all look different.
Some sassafras leaves look like footballs.
Some look like mittens. And some look
like ghosts! And the roots of a sassafras
smell like root beer!

Sniff!
Sniff!

I saw a
sassafras

place your
sticker here

White Oak

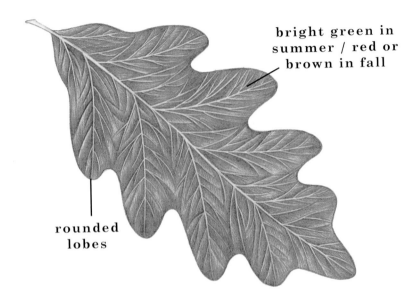

bright green in
summer / red or
brown in fall

rounded
lobes

There are many kinds of oak trees.
And many kinds of oak leaves.
Most oaks belong to the white oak
family or the red oak family.
White oak leaves are large and have
rounded lobes.

You know you are looking at an oak tree if you see acorns. Acorns are the fruit of an oak tree. But you cannot eat them!

I saw a
white oak

place your
sticker here

Red Oak

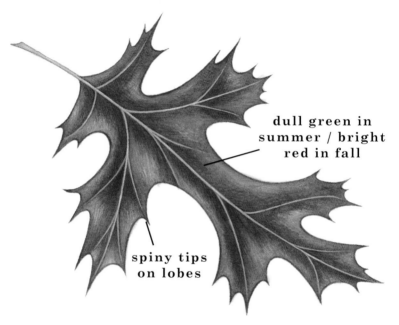

dull green in
summer / bright
red in fall

spiny tips
on lobes

Red oaks have long leaves
with sharp, pointy lobes.

In the fall, red oaks have
bright autumn leaves that
look like red-hot flames
of fire!

I saw a
red oak

place your
sticker here

Maple

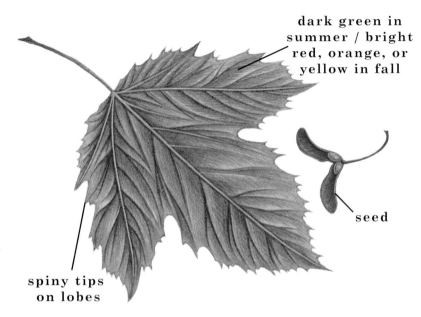

dark green in summer / bright red, orange, or yellow in fall

seed

spiny tips on lobes

There are many kinds of maple trees.
But their leaves all look a lot alike.
This leaf is from a red maple tree.
It can have three or five lobes—
all covered with jagged teeth.

 Maple syrup comes from the sugar maple tree.

All maple trees have seeds
that look like pairs of wings.
Toss a maple seed into the air.
It twirls to the ground
like a little helicopter.
On a windy day,
the seed blows away.
It will grow into another tree!

I saw a
maple

place your
sticker here

Sweetgum

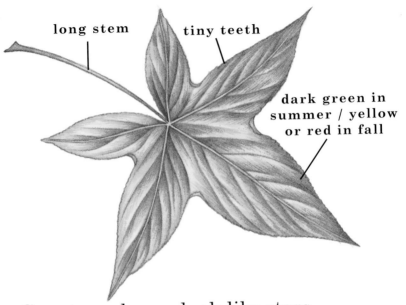

long stem

tiny teeth

dark green in summer / yellow or red in fall

Sweetgum leaves look like stars.
They have a strong, sweet smell
when you rub them.
You may also see
prickly balls like this.
They are the
sweetgum's fruit.
There are seeds inside.

The sweetgum gets its name
from the thick sap in its trunk.
Long ago, people chewed it just like gum!

I saw a
sweetgum

place your
sticker here

Honey Locust

shiny, dark green
in summer /
yellow in fall

tiny oval
leaflets

The honey locust leaf
looks like a branch
with lots of little leaves.
But this is just one big leaf
with lots of leaflets.
One leaf can have
more than 100 leaflets!

pod with
seeds inside

I saw a
honey locust

place your
sticker here

Black Walnut

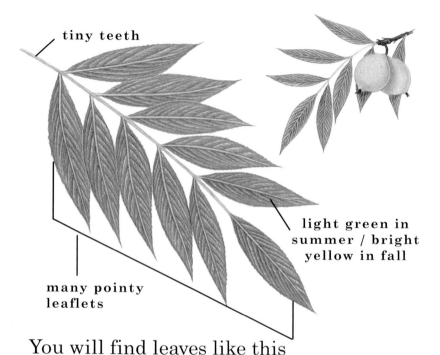

tiny teeth

light green in
summer / bright
yellow in fall

many pointy
leaflets

You will find leaves like this
on many kinds of nut trees.
If you find a black walnut leaf,
look for walnut husks, too.
Inside are walnuts.
The thick husks can turn
your hands brown!

I saw a
black walnut

place your
sticker here

Buckeye

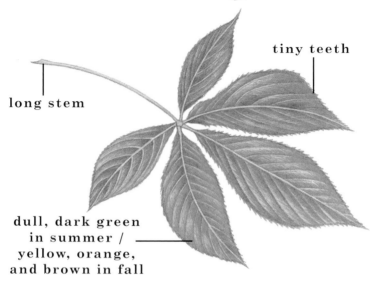

tiny teeth

long stem

dull, dark green
in summer /
yellow, orange,
and brown in fall

Buckeye leaves spread out
like pointy fingers on a hand.
Sometimes they have five leaflets.
And sometimes they have seven.
Buckeye trees have
pretty flowers in the spring
and nuts in the fall.
But do not eat them!
They are poisonous.

Leave It to You

When you have collected
all kinds of leaves,
in all kinds of shapes,
and all kinds of colors,
put them together.
Glue them on a piece of paper
and make a leaf picture!

I saw a
buckeye

place your
sticker here

Now you know about
lots of leaves and trees.
But this is only the beginning!
To see more leaves and trees,
take a trip to a tree farm
or a plant nursery.
Or see if there is
a botanical garden nearby.
This is like a plant museum.
You will see trees from all over the world!

Looking at Trees and Leaves

My Field Notes

*Use these pages to write down or draw what you see when you are looking at leaves and trees. Write the name of each leaf and describe it.

*Don't forget: Describe the leaf in your notes even if you can't tell from this book what kind it is. Maybe later you will see the leaf or the tree it belongs to in another book!

Today's date: _____

Leaf number: _____

Kind of leaf: _____

Shape: _____

Size: _____

Where I found it: _____

My notes: _____

_____

_____

_____

_____

You can draw here!

Today's date:

Leaf number:

Kind of leaf:

Shape:

Size:

Where I found it:

My notes:

You can draw here!

Today's date:

Leaf number:

Kind of leaf:

Shape:

Size:

Where I found it:

My notes:

You can draw here!

Today's date:

Leaf number:

Kind of leaf:

Shape:

Size:

Where I found it:

My notes:

You can draw here!

Today's date:

Leaf number:

Kind of leaf:

Shape:

Size:

Where I found it:

My notes:

You can draw here!

Today's date:

Leaf number:

Kind of leaf:

Shape:

Size:

Where I found it:

My notes:

You can draw here!

Today's date:

Leaf number:

Kind of leaf:

Shape:

Size:

Where I found it:

My notes:

You can draw here!